Christening Sets
for Him & Her™

General Information

Many of the products used in this pattern book can be purchased from local craft, fabric and variety stores, or from the Annie's Attic Needlecraft Catalog (see Customer Service information on page 15).

Contents

Gift From Heaven
Christening Ensemble

DESIGNED BY JOYCE NORDSTROM

SKILL LEVEL

INTERMEDIATE

FINISHED SIZES

Instructions given for jacket and shorts fit size 3 months, changes for 6, 12, 18 and 24 months are in [ ].

Instructions given for hat fit sizes 3–6 months, changes for 12–24 months are in [ ].

Booties and afghan are 1 size only.

FINISHED GARMENT MEASUREMENTS

Chest: 19 [20, 21, 22, 23] inches
Afghan: 36 x 36 inches

MATERIALS

- Lion Brand Babysoft fine (sport) weight yarn (5 oz/459 yds/141g per skein):
  6 skeins #100 crisp white
- Size F/5/3.75mm crochet hook or size needed to obtain gauge (for jacket, shorts, booties & hat)
- Size G/6/4mm crochet hook or size needed to obtain gauge (for afghan)
- Tapestry needle
- 4 yds off-white ⅛-inch wide satin ribbon
- 4 [4, 5, 5] white ⅝-inch buttons
- Sewing needle and matching thread

GAUGE

Size F hook: 16 hdc = 4 inches
Size G hook: Motif = 5 inches
Take time to check gauge.

PATTERN NOTES

Weave in ends as work progresses.

Join with slip stitch as indicated unless otherwise stated.

Chain-3 at beginning of rounds counts as a double crochet unless otherwise stated.

Chain-4 at beginning of rounds counts as a double crochet and a chain-1 space unless otherwise stated.

JACKET

Note: *Jacket Back, Fronts and Sleeves are worked lengthwise and in* **back lps** *(see Stitch Guide) only.*

BACK

Foundation row (RS): Ch 46 [48, 50, 52, 54], hdc in 3rd ch from hook, hdc in each rem ch across, turn. *(44 [46, 48, 50, 52] hdc)*

Row 1: Ch 2, hdc in each hdc across, turn.

Rep row 1 until piece measures 9½ [10, 10½, 11, 11½] inches from beg. At end of last row, fasten off.

RIGHT FRONT

Foundation row (RS): Beg at neck edge, ch 31 [33, 35, 37, 39], hdc in 3rd ch from hook, hdc in each rem ch across, turn. *(29 [31, 33, 35, 37] hdc)*

Row 1: Ch 2, hdc in each hdc to last hdc, 2 hdc in last hdc, turn. *(30 [32, 34, 36, 38] hdc)*

Row 2: Ch 2, 2 hdc in first hdc, hdc in each rem hdc across, turn. *(31 [33, 35, 37, 39] hdc)*

Row 3: Ch 2, hdc in each hdc to last hdc, 2 hdc in last hdc, turn. *(32 [34, 36, 38, 40] hdc)*

Rows 4–9 [4–11, 4–13, 4–15, 4–17]: [Rep rows 2 and 3 alternately] 3 [4, 5, 6, 7] times. *(38 [40, 42, 44, 46] hdc at end of last row)*

RIGHT SHOULDER

Row 1: Ch 8, hdc in 3rd ch from hook, hdc in each of next 5 chs, hdc in each rem hdc across, turn. *(44 [46, 48, 50, 52] hdc)*

Row 2: Ch 2, hdc in each hdc across, turn.

Rep row 2 until piece measures 5¼ [5½, 5¾, 6, 6¼] inches from beg. At end of last row, fasten off.

LEFT FRONT

Foundation row (RS): Ch 31 [33, 35, 37, 39], hdc in 3rd ch from hook, hdc in each rem ch across, turn. *(29 [31, 33, 35, 37] hdc)*

Row 1: Ch 2, 2 hdc in first hdc, *ch 1 *(buttonhole)*, sk next hdc, hdc in next 7 hdc, rep from * twice, ch 1 *(buttonhole)*, sk next hdc, hdc in each rem hdc, turn. *(30 [32, 34, 36, 38] sts, 4 ch-1 sps)*

Row 2: Ch 2, hdc in each st to last hdc, 2 hdc in last hdc, turn. *(31 [33, 35, 37, 39] hdc)*

Row 3: Ch 2, 2 hdc in first hdc, hdc in each rem hdc across, turn. *(32 [34, 36, 38, 40] hdc)*

Rows 4–9 [4–11, 4–13, 4–15, 4–17]: [Rep rows 2 and 3 alternately] 3 [4, 5, 6, 7] times. *(38 [40, 42, 44, 46] hdc at end of last row)*

LEFT SHOULDER

Row 1: Ch 8, hdc in 3rd ch from hook, hdc in each of next 5 chs, hdc in each rem hdc across, turn. *(44 [46, 48, 50, 52] hdc)*

Row 2: Ch 2, hdc in each hdc across, turn.

Rep row 2 until piece measures 5¼ [5½, 5¾, 6, 6¼] inches from beg. At end of last row, fasten off.

SLEEVE
Make 2.

Foundation row: Ch 30 [32, 36, 38, 40], hdc in 3rd ch from hook, hdc in each rem ch to last 5 chs, sc in each of last 5 chs, turn. *(23 [25, 29, 31, 33] hdc)*

Row 1: Ch 1, sc in each of first 5 sc, hdc in each hdc across, turn.

Row 2: Ch 2, hdc in each hdc, sc in each sc across, turn.

Rep rows 1 and 2 alternately until piece measures 7¼, [7¾, 8¼, 8¾, 9¼] inches from beg. At end of last row, fasten off.

ASSEMBLY
Sew shoulder seams, matching shoulders of fronts to shoulder edge of back and leaving center of back unsewn for back neck edge.

EDGING
Row 1: Hold Jacket with RS facing, **join** *(see Pattern Notes on page 2)* yarn at lower edge of Right Front, sc evenly up Right Front, 3 sc at neck edge corner, sc evenly around neck edge, across back, down Left Front neck edge, 3 sc at neck edge corner, sc evenly down Left Front, taking care to keep edges flat, turn.

Note: *For buttonholes on Edging, mark sc on row 1 to correspond to buttonholes on Left Front.*

Row 2: Ch 2, [hdc in each sc to first marked sc, ch 1 *(buttonhole)*, sk marked sc] 4 times, hdc in each sc to 2nd sc of next corner, 3 hdc in 2nd sc, hdc in each sc to 2nd sc of next corner, 3 hdc in 2nd sc, hdc in each rem sc, turn.

Row 3: Ch 1, sc in each hdc to 2nd hdc of next corner, 3 sc in 2nd hdc, sc in each hdc to 2nd hdc of next corner, 3 sc in 2nd sc, sc in each rem hdc and in each ch-1 sp. Fasten off.

FINISHING
Sew buttons to Right Front matching buttonholes on Left Front.

SHORTS
Note: *Shorts are worked in 1 piece from back seam to back seam and in back lps only.*

LEFT LEG
Row 1: Ch 40 [42, 44, 46, 48], hdc in 3rd ch from hook, hdc in each of next 29 [31, 33, 35, 37] chs, sc in each of last 8 chs, turn. *(38 [40, 42, 44, 46] sts)*

Row 2: Ch 1, sc in each of first 8 sc, hdc in each hdc to last hdc, 2 hdc in last hdc, turn. *(39 [41, 43, 45, 47] sts)*

Row 3: Ch 2, 2 hdc in first hdc, hdc in each hdc, sc in each sc, turn. *(40 [42, 44, 46, 48] sts)*

Row 4: Ch 1, sc in each of first 8 sc, hdc in each hdc to last hdc, 3 hdc in last hdc, turn. *(42 [44, 46, 48, 50] sts)*

Row 5: Ch 5, sc in 2nd ch from hook, sc in each of next 2 chs, hdc in next ch, hdc in each rem hdc, sc in each sc, turn. *(46 [48, 50, 52, 54] sts)*

Row 6: Ch 1, sc in each of first 8 sc, hdc in each hdc to last 3 hdc, sc in each of last 3 hdc, turn.

Row 7: Ch 1, sc in each of first 3 sc, hdc in each hdc, sc in each sc, turn.

Rep rows 6 and 7 alternately until piece measures 8½ [8¾, 9, 9¼, 9¾] from beg.

WAISTBAND
Row 1: Ch 1, sc in each of first 8 sc, hdc each hdc to last 4 sts, leaving rem sts unworked, turn. *(42 [44, 46, 48, 50] sts)*

Row 2: Ch 2, hdc first hdc, [yo, draw up lp in next hdc] 3 times, yo and draw through all 7 lps on hook, hdc in each rem hdc, sc in each sc, turn. *(40 [42, 44, 46, 48] sts)*

Row 3: Ch 1, sc in each of first 8 sc, hdc in each hdc to last 2 hdc, **hdc dec** *(see Stitch Guide)* in last 2 hdc, turn. *(39 [41, 43, 45, 47] sts)*

Row 4: Ch 2, hdc dec in first 2 hdc, hdc in each rem hdc, sc in each sc, turn. *(38 [40, 42, 44, 46] sts)*

Row 5: Ch 1, sc in each of first 8 sc, hdc in each hdc, turn.

RIGHT LEG
Row 1: Ch 2, hdc in each hdc, sc in each sc, turn.

Row 2: Ch 1, sc in each of first 8 sc, hdc in each hdc to last hdc, 2 hdc in last hdc, turn. *(39 [41, 43, 45, 47] sts)*

Row 3: Ch 2, 2 hdc in first hdc, hdc in each hdc, sc in each sc, turn. *(40 [42, 44, 46, 48] sts)*

Row 4: Ch 1, sc in each of first 8 sc, hdc in each hdc to last hdc, 3 hdc in last hdc, turn. *(42 [44, 46, 48, 50] sts)*

Row 5: Ch 5, sc in 2nd ch from hook, sc in each of next 2 chs, hdc in next ch, hdc in each rem hdc, sc in each sc, turn. *(46 [48, 50, 52, 54] sts)*

Row 6: Ch 1, sc in each of first 8 sc, hdc in each hdc to last 3 hdc, sc in each of last 3 hdc, turn.

Row 7: Ch 1, sc in each of first 3 sc, hdc in each hdc, sc in each sc, turn.

Rep rows 6 and 7 alternately until piece measures 8½ [8¾, 9, 9¼, 9¾] from beg.

WAISTBAND
Row 1: Ch 1, sc in each of first 8 sc, hdc each hdc to last 4 sts, leaving rem sts unworked, turn. *(42 [44, 46, 48, 50] sts)*

Row 2: Ch 2, hdc first hdc, [yo, draw up lp in next hdc] 3 times, yo and draw through all 7 lps on hook, hdc in each rem hdc, sc in each sc, turn. *(40 [42, 44, 46, 48] sts)*

Row 3: Ch 1, sc in each of first 8 sc, hdc in each hdc to last 2 hdc, hdc dec in last 2 hdc, turn. *(39 [41, 43, 45, 47] sts)*

Row 4: Ch 2, hdc dec in first 2 hdc, hdc in each rem hdc, sc in each sc, turn. *(38 [40, 42, 44, 46] sts)*

Row 5: Ch 1, sc in each of first 8 sc, hdc in each hdc. Fasten off.

ASSEMBLY

Folding piece in half, sew beg ch of Left Leg to last short row of Right Leg to form back seam. Refold and sew inseams from end of 1 Leg to end of other Leg.

BUTTON LOOPS

Join yarn in approximate right front of waist band, ch 4, sk next 2 ribs of waist band, sc in next rib. Fasten off and weave in ends.

Rep for other button lp on left side of front.

SUSPENDER

Make 2.

Row 1: Ch 54 [58, 62, 66, 70], hdc in 3rd ch from hook, hdc in each rem ch across, turn. *(52 [56, 60, 64, 68] hdc)*

Row 2: Ch 2, hdc in each hdc across, turn.

Row 3: Ch 2, hdc in each hdc across. Fasten off.

FINISHING

Step 1: Sew 1 end of each Suspender at back of Shorts.

Step 2: Sew buttons in place at opposite ends of Suspenders.

HAT
BORDER

Row 1 (RS): Ch 57 [61], sc in 2nd ch from hook, sc in each rem ch across, turn. *(56 [60] sc)*

Row 2: Ch 1, working in **back lps** *(see Stitch Guide)* only, sc in each sc across, turn.

Rep row 2 until piece measures 2½ inches from beg.

CROWN

Row 1: Ch 2, working in back lps only, hdc in first sc, hdc in each rem sc across, turn

Row 2: Ch 2, hdc in each hdc across, turn.

Rep row 2 until piece measures 5½ inches from beg.

TOP SHAPING

Row 1: Ch 2, hdc in each of first 3 hdc, hdc dec in next 2 hdc, *hdc in each of next 3 hdc, hdc dec in next 2 hdc, rep from * across, turn. *(40 [50] hdc)*

Row 2: Ch 2, hdc in each of first 5 hdc, hdc in next 2 hdc, *hdc in each of next 5 hdc, hdc dec in next 2 hdc, rep from * to last 5 [1] hdc, hdc in last 5 [1] hdc, turn. *(35 [43] hdc)*

Row 3: Ch 2, hdc in each of first 4 hdc, hdc dec in next 2 hdc, *hdc in each of next 4 hdc, hdc dec in next 2 hdc, rep from * to last 5 [1] hdc, hdc in last 5 [1] hdc, turn. *(30 [36] hdc)*

Row 4: Ch 2, hdc in each of first 3 hdc, hdc dec in next 2 hdc, *hdc in each of next 3 hdc, hdc dec in next 2 hdc, rep from * to last 0 [1] hdc, hdc in last 0 [1] hdc, turn. *(24 [29] hdc)*

Row 5: Ch 2, hdc in each of first 2 hdc, hdc dec in next 2 hdc, *hdc in each of next 2 hdc, hdc dec in next 2 hdc, rep from * to last 0 [1] hdc, hdc in last 0 [1] hdc, turn. *(18 [22] hdc)*

Row 6: Ch 2, hdc in first hdc, hdc dec in next 2 hdc, *hdc in next hdc, hdc dec in next 2 hdc, rep from * to last 0 [1] hdc, hdc in last 0 [1] hdc. Fasten off, leaving a 15-inch end for sewing. *(12 [15] hdc)*

FINISHING

Draw up all rem sts tightly and carefully sew back seam.

BOOTIE
Make 2.

SOLE

Rnd 1 (RS): Ch 13, sc in 2nd ch from hook *(mark for heel)*, 2 sc in next ch, sc in each of next 8 chs, 2 sc in next ch, sc in last ch *(mark for toe)*, working on opposite side in unused lps of starting ch, 2 sc in next lp, sc in each of next 8 lps, 2 sc in next lp, join in back lp of beg sc. *(26 sc)*

***Note:** Mark end of rnds.*

Rnd 2: Ch 1, sc in same lp as joining, working in back lps only, 2 sc in next sc, sc in each of next 10 sc, 2 sc in next sc, sc in each of next sc, 2 sc in next sc, sc in each of next 10 sc, 2 sc in next sc, join in back lp of beg sc. *(30 sc)*

Rnd 3: Ch 1, sc in same lp as joining, working in back lps only, 2 sc in next sc, sc in each of next 12 sc, 2 sc in next sc, sc in next sc, 2 sc in next sc, sc in each of next 12 sc, 2 sc in next sc, join in back lp of beg sc. *(34 sc)*

Rnd 4: Ch 1, sc in same lp as joining, working in back lps only, 2 sc in next sc, sc in each of next 14 sc, 2 sc in next sc, sc in next sc, 2 sc in next sc, sc in each of next 14 sc, 2 sc in next sc, join in back lp of beg sc. *(38 sc)*

Rnd 5: Ch 1, sc in same lp as joining, working in back lps only, 2 sc in next sc, sc in each of next 16 sc, 2 sc in next sc, sc in next sc, 2 sc in next sc, sc in each of next 16 sc, 2 sc in next sc, join in back lp of beg sc. *(42 sc)*

FOOT

Rnd 1: Ch 2, hdc in same lp as joining, working in back lps only, hdc in each rem sc, join in 2nd ch of beg ch-2.

Rnd 2: Ch 2, hdc in each hdc, join in 2nd ch of beg ch-2.

Rnd 3: Rep rnd 2. Fasten off.

CUFF

Note: Mark center of heel.

Row 1 (WS): Hold piece with WS of heel end at top, join yarn in 8th hdc to right of center of heel, ch 2, hdc in same hdc, hdc in each of next 15 hdc, leaving rem hdc unworked, turn. *(16 hdc)*

Row 2 (RS): Ch 2, hdc in first hdc, hdc dec in next 2 hdc, hdc in each hdc across to last 3 hdc, hdc dec in next 2 hdc, hdc in last hdc, turn. *(14 hdc)*

Row 3: Rep row 2. *(12 hdc at end of row)*

Row 4: Ch 2, hdc in each hdc across, turn.

Row 5: Ch 2, hdc in each hdc across. Fasten off.

EDGING

Row 1 (RS): Hold piece with RS facing, join yarn in row 1 of Cuff, work 8 sc evenly sp to next corner, 3 sc in corner, sc in each st across back to next corner, 3 sc in corner, work 8 sc evenly sp across to end of row 1 of Cuff, turn.

Row 2: Ch 1, sc in first sc, [ch 1, sk next sc, sc in each of next 2 sc] twice, ch 1, sk next sc, sc in next sc, 3 sc in next sc, sc in each sc to 2nd sc of next corner, 3 sc in 2nd sc, sc in next sc, [ch 1, sk next sc, sc in each of next 2 sc] twice, ch 1, sk next sc, sc in last sc. Fasten off.

TONGUE

Work same as Sole.

TIE

MAKE 2.

With 2 strands held tog, ch 75. Fasten off.

ASSEMBLY

Pin center of toe of Tongue to center of toe of Foot. Matching sts from center to each side of Foot, pin sts tog. Working through double thickness at same time, work sc evenly around other side and around end of Tongue, join in beg sc. Fasten off.

FINISHING

Weave 1 Tie through row 2 of each Bootie.

AFGHAN
PLAIN MOTIF
Make 24.

Foundation row (RS): Ch 21, hdc in 3rd ch from hook, hdc in each rem ch across, turn. *(19 hdc)*

Row 1: Ch 2, hdc in each hdc across, turn.

Rep row 1 until piece measures 5 inches from beg.

EDGING

Ch 1, sc evenly sp around motif, working [sc, ch 1, sc] in each corner and 17 sc along each side, join in beg sc. Fasten off.

CIRCLE MOTIF
Make 25.

Rnd 1 (RS): Ch 5, join in first ch to form a ring, **ch 3** (see Pattern Notes on page 2), 15 dc in ring, join in 3rd ch of beg ch-3. (16 dc)

Rnd 2: **Ch 4** (see Pattern Notes on page 2), *dc in next dc, ch 1, rep from * around, join in 3rd ch of beg ch-4. (16 ch-1 sps)

Rnd 3: Ch 3, 2 dc in next ch-1 sp, [dc in next dc, 2 dc in next ch-1 sp] 5 times, join in 3rd ch of beg ch-3. (48 dc)

Rnd 4: Ch 1, sc in same ch as joining, *ch 5, sk next 2 dc, sc in next dc, [ch 3, sk next 2 dc, sc in next dc] 3 times, rep from * twice, ch 5, sk next 2 dc, sc in next dc, [ch 3, sk next 2 dc, sc in next dc] twice, ch 3, sk next 2 dc, join in beg sc.

Rnd 5: Sl st in next ch-5 sp, ch 3, 2 dc in same sp, *3 dc in each of next 3 ch-3 sps, (3 dc, ch 3, 3 dc) in next ch-5 sp (corner), rep from * twice, 3 dc in each of next 3 ch-3 sps, 3 dc in same sp as beg ch-3 made, ch 1, join with hdc in 3rd ch of beg ch-3.

Row 6: Ch 1, 2 sc in sp formed by joining hdc, *sc in each of next 15 dc, (2 sc, ch 1, 2 sc) in next ch-3 sp (corner), rep from * twice, sc in

each of next 15 dc, 2 sc in same sp as beg 2 sc made, ch 1, join in beg sc. Fasten off.

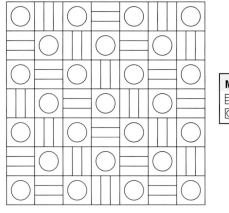

MOTIF KEY
⊞ Plain Motif
◎ Circle Motif

Gift from Heaven
Assembly Diagram

FINISHING
Referring to Assembly Diagram for placement, sew Motifs tog.

BORDER
Rnd 1: Join yarn in any corner ch-1 sp, ch 1, (sc, ch 2, sc) in same sp, *ch 1, sk next st, sc in next st, rep from * around, working (sc, ch 2, sc) in each rem corner ch-1 sp, join in beg sc.

Rnd 2: Sl st in next ch-1 sp, ch 2 (counts as a hdc), hdc in same sp, 2 hdc in each rem ch-1 sp around and working (2 hdc, ch 2, 2 hdc) in each corner ch-2 sp, join in 2nd ch of beg ch-2.

Rnd 3: Sl st in next hdc, ch 2 (counts as a hdc), hdc in same hdc, *sk next hdc, 2 hdc in next hdc, rep from * around, working (2 hdc, ch 2, 2 hdc) in each corner ch-2 sp, join with sl st in 2nd ch of beg ch-2.

Rnd 4: Rep rnd 3. At end of rnd, fasten off.

Rnd 5: Join yarn in any corner ch-2 sp, ch 1, (sc, ch 3, sc) in same sp, *ch 6, sk next 5 hdc, sc in next hdc, ch 3, sk next hdc, sc in next hdc, rep from * around, working (sc, ch 3, sc) in each rem corner ch-2 sp, join in beg sc.

Rnd 6: Sl st in each of next 3 chs, sl st in next sc, sl st in next next ch-6 sp, (3 dc, ch 3, sl st, ch 3, 3 dc) in same sp, (sl st, 3 dc, ch 3, sl st, ch 3, 3 dc) in each rem ch-6 sp around, sk first 4 sl sts, join in next sl st. Fasten off. ■

Love Knot
Layette

DESIGNED BY ELIZABETH ANN WHITE

SKILL LEVEL

INTERMEDIATE

BABY AFGHAN
FINISHED SIZE

28 inches x 36 inches

MATERIALS

- Fine (sport) weight pompadour yarn: 15 oz/1350 yds/425g white
- Size H/8/5mm crochet hook or size needed to obtain gauge
- Tapestry needle
- Sewing needle
- 4 yds white ½-inch wide satin ribbon
- 1⅓ yds white ¼-inch wide satin ribbon
- Matching sewing thread

2 FINE

GAUGE

(Sc, ch 1) = ½ inch; rows 1–4 = 1 inch
Take time to check gauge.

PATTERN NOTES

Weave in ends as work progresses.

Join with slip stitch as indicated unless otherwise stated.

Chain-3 at beginning of rounds counts as a double crochet unless otherwise

Chain-4 at beginning of rounds counts as a double crochet and a chain-1 space unless otherwise stated.

SPECIAL STITCHES

Double love knot (dlk): Draw up long lp on hook to measure ¾ inch, yo, draw through lp on hook, sc in back strand of long lp (*see Fig. 1*), draw up long lp, yo, draw through lp on hook, sc in back strand of long lp (*see Fig. 2*).

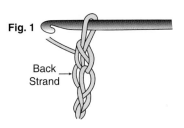

Fig. 1

Back Strand →

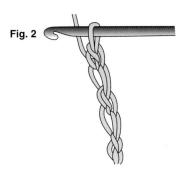

Fig. 2

Love knot (lk): Draw up long lp on hook to measure ¾ inch, yo, draw through lp on hook, sc in back strand of long lp.

AFGHAN

Row 1 (RS): Ch 82, sc in 2nd ch from hook, *ch 1, sk next ch, sc in next ch, rep from * across, turn. (*41 sc*)

Row 2: Ch 1, sc in first sc, *ch 1, sk next ch-1 sp, sc in next sc, rep from * across, turn.

Rows 3–101: Rep row 2.

BORDER

Rnd 1: Ch 4, [dc, ch 1] twice in first sc (*beg corner*), sk next ch-1 sp, *dc in next sc, ch 1, sk next ch-1 sp, rep from * across to last sc, [dc, ch 1] 3 times in last sc (*corner*), working across

next side, sk next row, *dc in end of next row, ch 1, sk next row, rep from * across, working across next side in unused lps of starting ch, [dc, ch 1] 3 times in first ch *(corner)*, sk next ch, *dc in next ch, ch 1, sk next ch, rep from * across to last ch, [dc, ch 1] 3 times in last ch *(corner)*, working across next side, sk next row, *dc in end of next row, ch 1, sk next row, rep from * across to beg ch-4, **join** *(see Pattern Notes on page 9)* in 3rd ch of beg ch-4.

Rnd 2: Sl st in next ch, sl st in next dc, ch 1, (sc, **dlk**—*see Special Stitches*, sc) in same dc *(corner)*, dlk, sk next ch-1 sp, *sc in next dc, dlk, sk next ch-1 sp, * rep from * across to 2nd dc of next corner, (sc, dlk, sc) in 2nd dc of corner *(corner)*, sk next dc, dlk, sk next ch-1 sp, **sc in next dc, dlk, sk next ch-1 sp, * rep from ** across to 2nd dc of next corner, (sc, dlk, sc) in 2nd dc of corner *(corner)*, sk next dc, dlk, sk next ch-1 sp, ***sc in next dc, dlk, sk next ch-1 sp, * rep from *** across to 2nd dc of next corner, (sc, dlk, sc) in 2nd dc of corner *(corner)*, sk next dc, dlk, sk next ch-1 sp, ****sc in next ch-1 sp, dlk, sk next ch-1 sp, rep from * across to beg sc, join in beg sc.

Rnd 3: Lk *(see Special Stitches)*, (sc, dlk, sc) in center of next dlk, dlk, *sc in center of next dlk, dlk, rep from * across to dlk of next corner, *(sc, dlk, sc) in dlk *(corner)*, dlk, *sc in center of next dlk, dlk, rep from * across to dlk of next corner, rep from * around, join in beg sc.

Rnds 4–7: Rep rnd 3. At end of last rnd, fasten off.

FINISHING

Weave ½-inch ribbon through sts of rnd 1 of Border. Trim and tack ends together. Cut ¼-inch ribbon into 4 pieces; tie each piece into bow. Tack 1 bow at each corner of rnd 1 of Border.

GOWN
FINISHED SIZE
Fits newborn–3 months.

MATERIALS
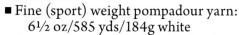
- Fine (sport) weight pompadour yarn: 6½ oz/585 yds/184g white
- Size 0/2.50mm steel crochet hook or size needed to obtain gauge
- Tapestry needle
- Sewing needle
- 2 yds white ¼-inch wide satin ribbon
- 2 small white ribbon roses
- 3 white 10mm buttons
- Matching sewing thread

GAUGE
5 dc = 1 inch; 3 dc rows = 1 inch
Take time to check gauge.

GOWN
Row 1 (RS): Starting at neck opening, ch 55, dc in 4th ch from hook *(beg 3 sk chs count as a dc)*, dc in each of next 6 chs, ch 2, dc in each of next 12 chs, ch 2, dc in each of next 13 chs, ch 2, dc in each of next 12 chs, ch 2, dc in each of last 8 chs, turn. *(53 dc, 4 ch-2 sps)*

Row 2: Ch 3 *(see Pattern Notes on page 9)*, dc in each st across with (2 dc, ch 2, 2 dc) in each ch-2 sp, turn.

Rows 3 & 4: Rep row 2. *(101 dc at end of last row)*

Row 5: Ch 3, dc in each of next 13 dc, 2 dc in next ch-2 sp, ch 10 *(armhole)*, sk next 24 dc, 2 dc in next ch-2 sp, dc in each of next 25 dc, 2 dc in next ch-2 sp, ch 10 *(armhole)*, sk next 24 dc, 2 dc in next ch-2 sp, dc in each of last 14 dc, turn. *(61 dc, 2 ch-10 sps)*

Row 6: Ch 3, dc in each st and in each ch across, turn. *(81 dc)*

BORDER
Rnd 1: Ch 4 *(see Pattern Notes on page 9)*, sk next dc, *dc in next dc, ch 1, sk next dc, rep from * across, **join** *(see Pattern Notes on page 9)* in 3rd ch of beg ch-4, turn.

Rnd 2: Ch 3, 2 dc in next ch-1 sp, *dc in next dc, 2 dc in next ch-1 sp, rep from * around, join in 3rd ch of beg ch-3, turn.

Rnd 3: Ch 3, dc in each dc around, join in 3rd ch of beg ch-3, turn.

Rnds 4–41: Rep rnd 3. At end of last rnd, fasten off.

OVERSKIRT
Rnd 1 (RS): Hold piece with RS facing, join yarn with sc around **post** *(see Stitch Guide)* of first st on rnd 7, ***dlk** *(see Special Stitches on page 9)*, sc around post of next st on rnd 7, rep from * around, join in beg sc.

Rnd 2: Lk *(see Special Stitches on page 9)*, sc in center of first dlk, dlk, *sc in center of next dlk, dlk, rep from * around, join in beg sc.

Rnds 3–25: Rep rnd 2. At end of last rnd, fasten off.

PLACKETS
FIRST PLACKET
Working on 1 side of back opening, join yarn in end of row 1 of Gown, ch 3, 2 dc in end of same row, 2 dc in end of next row, [3 dc in end of next row, 2 dc in end of next row] twice. Fasten off.

2ND PLACKET
Working on opposite side of back opening, join yarn in end of row 6, ch 3, 2 dc in end of same row, 2 dc in end of next row, [3 dc in end of next row, 2 dc in end of next row] twice. Fasten off.

SLEEVE
Rnd 1 (RS): Hold 1 armhole with RS facing, join yarn with sc in first sk st on rnd 4, [dlk, sk next dc, sc in next dc] 11 times, dlk, sc in side of next dc on row 5, dlk, working in unused lps on opposite side of ch-10, sk next ch, sc in next ch, [dlk, sk next ch, sc in next ch] 4 times, dlk, sc in side of next dc on row 5, dlk, join in beg sc. *(19 dlk)*

Rnd 2: Lk, sc in center of first dlk, *sc in center of next dlk, dlk, rep from * around, join in beg sc.

Rnds 3–5: Rep rnd 2.

Rnd 6: Lk, sc in center of first dlk, sc in center of each dlk around, join in beg sc.

Rnd 7: Ch 1, sc in each st around, join in beg sc. Fasten off.

Rep on other armhole.

FINISHING
1: Sew buttons evenly spaced to one Placket.

2: Cut 2 pieces of 12-inch ribbon. Tie each piece in bow. Tack 1 bow to rnd 7 of each Sleeve.

3: Starting and ending at center front, weave rem ribbon through sts of rnd 7 of Gown. Tie ends in bow and trim.

4: Referring to photo for placement, sew ribbon roses to rows 1 and 4 of Gown.

SWEATER
FINISHED SIZE
Fits newborn–3 months.

MATERIALS
- Fine (sport) weight pompadour yarn: 3½ oz/315 yds/100g white
- Size 0/2.50mm steel crochet hook or size needed to obtain gauge
- Tapestry needle
- Sewing needle
- 40 inches white ¼-inch wide satin ribbon
- 4 small white ribbon roses
- Matching sewing thread

GAUGE
5 sc = 1 inch; 6 sc rows = 1 inch
Take time to check gauge.

SWEATER
Row 1 (RS): Ch 49, sc in 2nd ch from hook, sc in each rem ch across, turn. (48 sc)

Row 2: Ch 1, sc in each of first 6 sc, ch 2, [sc in each of next 12 sc, ch 2] 3 times, sc in each of last 6 sc, turn.

Row 3: Ch 1, sc in each st across with (sc, ch 2, sc) in each ch-2 sp, turn.

Rows 4–13: Rep row 3. (136 sc at end of last row)

Row 14: Ch 1, sc in each of first 17 sc, sc in next ch-2 sp, ch 10 (armhole), sk next 34 sc, sc in next ch-2 sp, sc in each of next 34 sc, sk next ch-2 sp, ch 10 (armhole), sk next 34 sc, sc in next ch-2 sp, sc in each of last 17 sc, turn. (71 sc, 2 ch-10 sps)

Row 15: Ch 1, sc in each sc and in each ch across, turn. (91 sc)

Row 16: Ch 1, sc in each sc across, turn.

Row 17: Ch 1, sc in first sc, **dlk** (see Special Stitches on page 9), sk next sc, sc in next sc, *dlk, sk next sc, sc in next sc, rep from * across, turn.

Row 18: 3 **Lk** (see Special Stitches on page 9), sc in center of first dlk, *dlk, sc in center of next dlk, rep from * across, turn.

Rows 19–26: Rep row 18. At end of last row, fasten off.

SLEEVE
Rnd 1: Hold 1 armhole with RS facing, join yarn with sc in first sk sc on row 13, [dlk, sk next sc, sc in next sc] 16 times, dlk, working in unused lps on opposite side of ch-10, sc in next ch, [dlk, sk next ch, sc in next ch] 4 times, dlk, **join** (see Pattern Notes on page 9) in beg sc. (22 dlk)

Rnd 2: Lk, sc in center of first dlk, dlk, *sc in center of next dlk, dlk, rep from * around, join in beg sc.

Rnds 3–8: Rep rnd 2.

Rnd 9: Lk, sc in center of first dlk, sc in center of each dlk around, join in beg lk.

Rnd 10: Ch 1, sc in each sc around, join in beg sc. Fasten off.

Rep on other armhole.

FINISHING
For ties, cut 4 pieces of 10-inch ribbon. Tack 1 tie to each side of row 2 and row 16 at front opening. Referring to photo for placement, tack 1 ribbon rose over end of each tie.

BONNET
FINISHED SIZE
Fits newborn–3 months.

MATERIALS
- Fine (sport) weight pompadour yarn: 2 oz/180 yds/56g white
- Size 0/2.50mm steel crochet hook or size needed to obtain gauge
- Tapestry needle
- Sewing needle
- 24 inches white ¼-inch wide satin ribbon
- 2 small white ribbon roses
- Matching sewing thread

GAUGE
5 dc = 1 inch; 3 dc rows = 1 inch
Take time to check gauge.

BONNET

Rnd 1 (RS): Ch 4, 11 dc in 4th ch from hook (*beg 3 sk chs count as a dc*), **join** (*see Pattern Notes on page 9*) in 3rd ch of beg 3 sk chs. (*12 dc*)

Rnd 2: Ch 3, dc in same ch as joining, 2 dc in each dc around, join in 3rd ch of beg ch-3. (*24 dc*)

Rnd 3: Ch 3, dc in same ch as joining, dc in next dc, [2 dc in next dc, dc in next dc] 11 times, join in 3rd ch of beg ch-3. (*36 dc*)

Rnd 4: Ch 3, dc in same ch as joining, dc in each of next 2 dc, [2 dc in next dc, dc in each of next 2 dc] 11 times, join in 3rd ch of beg ch-3. (*48 dc*)

Rnd 5: Ch 3, dc in same ch as joining, dc in each of next 3 dc, [2 dc in next dc, dc in each of next 3 dc] 11 times, join in 3rd ch of beg ch-3. (*60 dc*)

Row 6: Now working in rows, ch 1, sc in first st, **dlk** (*see Special Stitches on page 9*), sk next 2 dc, sc in next dc, [dlk, sk next 2 dc, sc in next dc] 12 times, leaving remaining sts unworked, turn. (*13 dlk, 14 sc*)

Row 7: 3 **Lk** (*see Special Stitches on page 9*), sc in center of first dlk, *dlk, sc in center of next dlk, rep from * across, turn.

Rows 8–11: Rep row 7.

Row 12: 3 Lk, sc in center of first dlk, *lk, sc in center of next dlk, rep from * across. Fasten off.

FINISHING

For ties, cut ribbon in 2 pieces each 12 inches long. Tack 1 tie to each end of row 12. Referring to photo, tack 1 ribbon rose over end of each tie.

BOOTIES
FINISHED SIZE

Fits newborn–3 months.

MATERIALS

- Fine (sport) weight pompadour yarn: 3 oz/270 yds/85g white
- Size 0/2.50mm steel crochet hook or size needed to obtain gauge
- Tapestry needle
- Sewing needle
- 24 inches white ¼-inch wide satin ribbon
- 2 small white ribbon roses
- Matching sewing thread

GAUGE

5 dc = 1 inch; 3 dc rows = 1 inch
Take time to check gauge.

BOOTIE
Make 2.

Rnd 1: Ch 4, **join** (*see Pattern Notes on page 9*) in first ch to form ring, **ch 3** (*see Pattern Notes on page 9*), 19 dc in ring, join in 3rd ch of beg ch-3. (*20 dc*)

Rnd 2: Ch 3, dc in each dc around, join in 3rd ch of beg ch-3.

Rnds 3 & 4: Rep rnd 2.

Row 5: Now working in rows, ch 3, dc in first st, dc in each dc across to last dc, 2 dc in last dc, turn.

Row 6: Ch 3, dc in each dc across, turn.

Rows 7–9: Rep row 6. At end of last row, fasten off.

ASSEMBLY

For center back seam, fold row 9 in half, working through both thicknesses at same time, join yarn in first st, sl st in each rem st across. Fasten off.

CUFF

Rnd 1: Working in ends of rows around top of Bootie, join yarn in row 9, **ch 4** (*see Pattern Notes on page 9*), dc in same row, ch 1, (dc, ch 1, dc, ch 1) in each row around, join in 3rd ch of beg ch-4.

Rnd 2: Sl st in next ch-1 sp, ch 1, (sc, **dlk**–*see Special Stitches on page 9* in same sp, (sc, dlk) in each rem ch-1 sp around, join in beg sc.

Rnd 3: Lk (*see Special Stitches on page 9*), sc in center of first dlk, lk, *sc in center of next lk, lk, rep from * around, join in beg st. Fasten off.

FINISHING

Cut 2 pieces of 12-inch ribbon. Starting and ending at center front, weave ribbon through sts of rnd 11. Tie ends in bow. Referring to photo for placement, tack 1 ribbon rose to each Bootie below bow. ■

American School of Needlework ®
excellence in instruction

TOLL-FREE ORDER LINE or to request a free catalog (800) 582-6643
Customer Service (800) 282-6643, **Fax** (800) 882-6643

Visit DRGnetwork.com.

We have made every effort to ensure the accuracy and completeness of these instructions.
We cannot, however, be responsible for human error, typographical mistakes or variations in individual work.

ISBN: 978-1-59012-225-9   All rights reserved.   Printed in USA   2 3 4 5 6 7 8 9

Stitch Guide

USA	Yarn Conversion	UK
Light Fingering		2 Ply
Fingering		3 Ply
Fingering/ Sport		4 Ply
Sport / Worsted Weight		Double Knitting
Bulky		Chunky
Bedspread Weight		Crochet No.10
Crochet Cotton		Crochet No.10

For more complete information, visit **FreePatterns.com**

ABBREVIATIONS

beg	begin/begins/beginning
bpdc	back post double crochet
bpsc	back post single crochet
bptr	back post treble crochet
CC	contrasting color
ch(s)	chain(s)
ch-	refers to chain or space previously made (i.e. ch-1 space)
ch sp(s)	chain space(s)
cl(s)	cluster(s)
cm	centimeter(s)
dc	double crochet (singular/plural)
dc dec	double crochet 2 or more stitches together, as indicated
dec	decrease/decreases/decreasing
dtr	double treble crochet
ext	extended
fpdc	front post double crochet
fpsc	front post single crochet
fptr	front post treble crochet
g	gram(s)
hdc	half double crochet
hdc dec	half double crochet 2 or more stitches together, as indicated
inc	increase/increases/increasing
lp(s)	loop(s)
MC	main color
mm	millimeter(s)
oz	ounce(s)
pc	popcorn(s)
rem	remain/remains/remaining
rep(s)	repeat(s)
rnd(s)	round(s)
RS	right side
sc	single crochet (singular/plural)
sc dec	single crochet 2 or more stitches together, as indicated
sk	skip/skipped/skipping
sl st(s)	slip stitch(es)
sp(s)	space(s)/spaced
st(s)	stitch(es)
tog	together
tr	treble crochet
trtr	triple treble
WS	wrong side
yd(s)	yard(s)
yo	yarn over

Chain—ch: Yo, pull through lp on hook.

Slip stitch—sl st: Insert hook in st, pull through both lps on hook.

Single crochet—sc: Insert hook in st, yo, pull through st, yo, pull through both lps on hook.

Front post stitch—fp: Back post stitch—bp: When working post st, insert hook from right to left around post st on previous row.

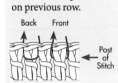

Front loop—front lp Back loop— back lp

Front Loop   Back Loop

Half double crochet— hdc: Yo, insert hook in st, yo, pull through st, yo, pull through all 3 lps on hook.

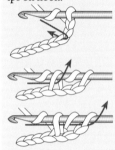

Double crochet—dc: Yo, insert hook in st, yo, pull through st, [yo, pull through 2 lps] twice.

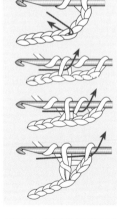

Change colors: Drop first color; with 2nd color, pull through last 2 lps of st.

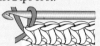

Treble crochet—tr: Yo twice, insert hook in st, yo, pull through st, [yo, pull through 2 lps] 3 times.

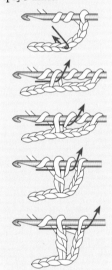

Double treble crochet—dtr: Yo 3 times, insert hook in st, yo, pull through st, [yo, pull through 2 lps] 4 times.

Single crochet decrease (sc dec): (Insert hook, yo, draw lp through) in each of the sts indicated, yo, draw through all lps on hook.

Example of 2-sc dec

Half double crochet decrease (hdc dec): (Yo, insert hook, yo, draw lp through) in each of the sts indicated, yo, draw through all lps on hook.

Example of 2-hdc dec

Double crochet decrease (dc dec): (Yo, insert hook, yo, draw loop through, draw through 2 lps on hook) in each of the sts indicated, yo, draw through all lps on hook.

Example of 2-dc dec

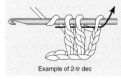

Example of 2-tr dec

Treble crochet decrease (tr dec): Holding back last lp of each st, tr in each of the sts indicated, yo, pull through all lps on hook.

US		UK
sl st (slip stitch)	=	sc (single crochet)
sc (single crochet)	=	dc (double crochet)
hdc (half double crochet)	=	htr (half treble crochet)
dc (double crochet)	=	tr (treble crochet)
tr (treble crochet)	=	dtr (double treble crochet)
dtr (double treble crochet)	=	ttr (triple treble crochet)
skip	=	miss